Union Public Library
1980 Morris Avenue
Union, N.J. 07083

P9-DBT-137

No Backbone!
The World of Invertebrates

Deadly Black Widows

Union Public Library
1980 Morris Avenue
Union, N.J. 07083

by Natalie Lunis

Consultant: Brian V. Brown
Curator, Entomology Section
Natural History Museum of Los Angeles County

BEARPORT
PUBLISHING

NEW YORK, NEW YORK

Credits

Cover, © John Cancalosi/Ardea; 4-5, © Ken Lucas/Ardea; 6, © Steve Maslowski/Visuals Unlimited/Getty Images; 7, © Jacob/Shutterstock; 8, © Bill Beatty/Visuals Unlimited/Getty Images; 9, © Stephen Dalton/Minden Pictures; 11, © John Giustina/VEER/Photonica/Getty Images; 12, © John A.L. Cooke/Animals Animals Earth Scenes; 13, © Bryan Reynolds/Phototake Inc./Alamy; 15, © Heidi & Hans-Jurgen Koch/Minden Pictures; 16T, © Dwight Kuhn/Dwight Kuhn Photography; 16C, © George Dodge/Bruce Coleman; 16B, © George Dodge/Bruce Coleman; 17, © Bryan Reynolds/Phototake Inc./Alamy; 18, © James Robinson/Animals Animals Earth Scenes; 19, © David Liebman Photography; 21, © George Grall/National Geographic/Getty Images; 22TL, © Sturgis McKeever, Georgia Southern University, United States; 22TR, © 2005 Jeff Hollenbeck; 22BL, © Ian Waldie/Getty Images; 22BR, © K. Korlevic; 23TL, © Jim Wehtje/Photodisc Green/Getty Images; 23TR, © Dwight Kuhn/Dwight Kuhn Photography; 23BL, © Bryan Reynolds/Phototake Inc./Alamy; 23BR, © Snowleopard1/Istockphoto.com.

Publisher: Kenn Goin
Editorial Director: Adam Siegel
Creative Director: Spencer Brinker
Design: Dawn Beard Creative
Photo Researcher: Beaura Kathy Ringrose

Library of Congress Cataloging-in-Publication Data

Lunis, Natalie.
  Deadly black widows / by Natalie Lunis.
     p. cm.—(No backbone! The world of invertebrates)
  Includes bibliographical references and index.
  ISBN-13: 978-1-59716-667-6 (library binding)
  ISBN-10: 1-59716-667-7 (library binding)
  1. Black widow spider—Juvenile literature. I. Title.

  QL458.42.T54L86 2009
  595.4'4—dc22

                      2008001997

Copyright © 2009 Bearport Publishing Company, Inc. All rights reserved. No part of this publication may be reproduced in whole or in part, stored in any retrieval system, or transmitted in any form or by any means, electronic, mechanical, photocopying, recording, or otherwise, without written permission from the publisher.

For more information, write to Bearport Publishing Company, Inc., 101 Fifth Avenue, Suite 6R, New York, New York 10003. Printed in the United States of America.

10 9 8 7 6 5 4 3 2

Contents

Danger— Black Widow!

Most **spiders** are not harmful to people.

The black widow, however, can kill a person.

It is the most dangerous spider in the United States.

This little black spider lives in every state except Alaska.

Most people who are
bitten by black widows
do not die. They do get
very sick, however.

A Black Widow's Body

Like all spiders, black widows have two main body parts.

The front part of the spider's body is a head and chest that are joined together.

The spider's eight legs are attached to this front part.

The back part contains the spider's heart, lungs, and tubes that it uses to make silk thread.

On a female black widow, the back part has a red hourglass shape on the bottom.

red hourglass

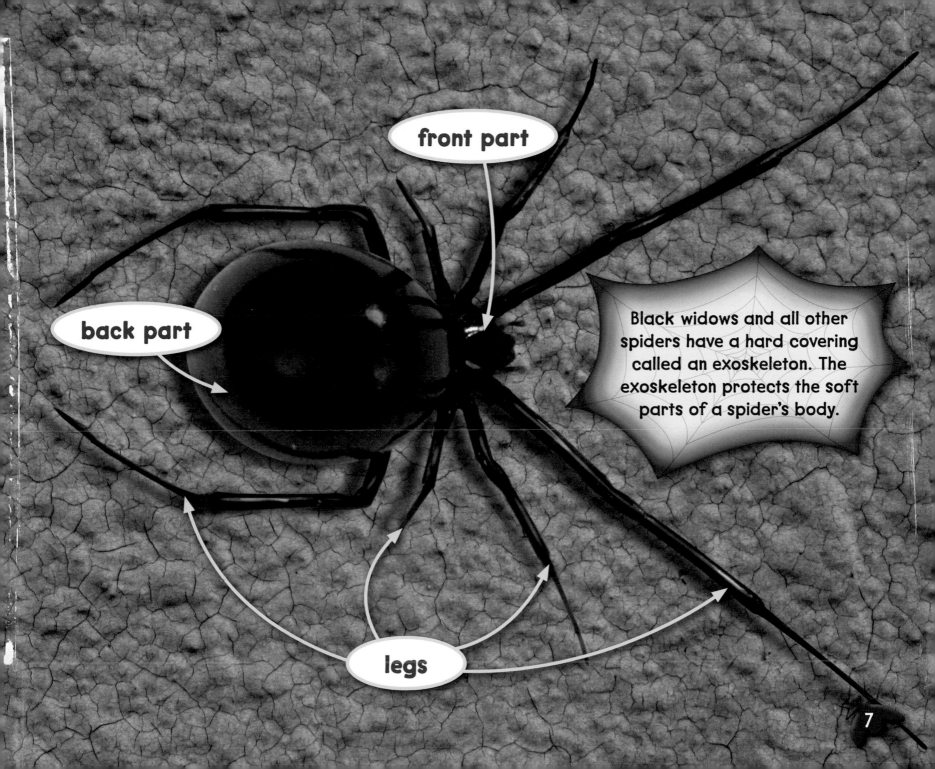

front part

back part

legs

Black widows and all other spiders have a hard covering called an exoskeleton. The exoskeleton protects the soft parts of a spider's body.

A Tangled Web

Black widow spiders make messy-looking webs to trap insects.

The webs are made out of silk thread.

The thread starts out as a liquid.

It comes out of little tubes that stick out of the spider's body.

As soon as the liquid hits the air, it dries.

The spider can now walk back and forth to weave its tangled web.

The tubes that shoot out the spider's silk thread are called spinnerets.

spinnerets

web

A Tricky Trap

The tangled, messy-looking web that a black widow makes is called a cobweb.

The black widow waits in its cobweb after weaving it.

In time, insects fly or crawl into the web and get stuck.

Then the black widow rushes over for a meal.

A black widow spider has eight eyes, yet it cannot see well. The spider knows that an insect has been caught when it feels its web shake.

cobweb

Mushy Meals

A black widow uses its fangs to bite and poison a trapped insect.

The spider's poison keeps its victim from moving.

The spider also spits juices from its stomach onto the insect.

These juices turn the soft parts of the insect into a soupy liquid.

The spider sucks up this liquid.

It needs to eat this way because it has no teeth for chewing!

Becoming a Widow

Insects are a black widow's main food.

Once in a while, however, a female black widow eats a male black widow after mating.

That's how the black widow got its name.

A widow is a woman whose husband has died.

When two spiders mate, they come together so the female can lay eggs that will hatch into young spiders.

male black widow

female black widow

Tiny Spiders

After mating, a female black widow lays hundreds of tiny eggs.

She makes an **egg sac** out of silk to protect them.

Tiny spiders, called **spiderlings**, come out of the eggs when they hatch.

They grow quickly inside the sac and shed their exoskeletons, which cannot stretch or grow.

Then they tear a hole in the egg sac and crawl off to start their lives in the outside world.

egg sac

eggs

spiderlings

eggs

A spider forms a new, bigger exoskeleton each time it sheds its old one. Shedding and forming a new exoskeleton is called molting.

spiderlings

Adult Life

Outside the egg sac, the little spiders keep growing.

Males and females grow differently, however.

Females molt eight or nine times.

Their bodies grow until they are around half an inch (1.3 cm) long—about the size of a raisin.

Males molt about five or six times and grow to be less than half the size of females.

female black widow

male black widow

praying mantis

Few animals eat adult black widows. However, young spiders are often eaten by birds, insects, and other kinds of spiders.

19

Deadly But Shy

Black widow spiders can be deadly.

Yet they are shy creatures.

They don't chase or attack people.

They will bite a person only if they feel bothered or threatened.

Luckily, these little spiders want to stay away from us as much as we want to stay away from them!

Sometimes black widows live in barns, houses, and other places near people. Most of the time, however, they live in out-of-the-way spots such as holes in the ground or rotten logs.

21

An animal that has a skeleton with a **backbone** inside its body is a *vertebrate* (VUR-tuh-brit). Mammals, birds, fish, reptiles, and amphibians are all vertebrates.

An animal that does not have a skeleton with a backbone inside its body is an *invertebrate* (in-VUR-tuh-brit). More than 95 percent of all kinds of animals on Earth are invertebrates.

Some invertebrates, such as insects and spiders, have hard skeletons—called exoskeletons—on the outside of their bodies. Other invertebrates, such as worms and jellyfish, have soft, squishy bodies with no exoskeletons to protect them.

Here are four spiders that are closely related to black widows. Like all spiders, they are invertebrates.

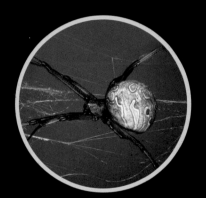

Brown Widow Spider

Red Widow Spider

Australian Redback Spider

Mediterranean Widow Spider

backbone
(BAK-*bohn*)
a group of
connected bones
that run along
the backs of some
animals, such as
dogs, cats, and fish;
also called a spine

egg sac
(EG SAK)
the silk container
that a female black
widow makes to
protect her eggs

spiderlings
(SPYE-dur-lingz)
baby spiders

spiders
(SPYE-durz)
small animals that
have eight legs,
two main body
parts, and a hard
covering called an
exoskeleton

Index

Read More

Ethan, Eric. *Black Widow Spiders*. Milwaukee, WI: Gareth Stevens Publishing (2004).

Murray, Peter. *Black Widows*. Chanhassen, MN: Child's World (2003).

Learn More Online

To learn more about black widow spiders, visit

www.bearportpublishing.com/NoBackbone-Spiders

About the Author

Natalie Lunis has written more than 30 science and nature books for children. She shares her home in the New York City area with several kinds of spiders—though hopefully not black widows.